A person's a person, no matter how small.

A person's a person, no matter how small.

TM & copyright © by Dr. Seuss Enterprises, L.P. 2018

All rights reserved.
Published in the United States by Random House Children's Books,
a division of Penguin Random House LLC, New York.
The artwork that appears herein was adapted from
Horton Hatches the Egg, TM & © 1940, renewed 1968 by Dr. Seuss Enterprises, L.P.;
Horton Hears a Who!, TM & © 1954, renewed 1982 by Dr. Seuss Enterprises, L.P., and
Horton and the Kwuggerbug and More Lost Stories, TM & © 2014 by Dr. Seuss Enterprises, L.P.

Random House and the colophon are registered trademarks of Penguin Random House LLC.

Visit us on the Web!
Seussville.com
rhcbooks.com

Educators and librarians, for a variety of teaching tools, visit us at
RHTeachersLibrarians.com

ISBN 978-0-525-58215-1

MANUFACTURED IN CHINA   10 9 8 7 6 5 4 3 2 1   First Edition

Dr. Seuss's

YOU ARE

KIND

featuring HORTON the ELEPHANT

Random House 🏠 New York

You are **KIND**.
You are an
amazing friend.

You always **LISTEN**.

If there's a problem,
you **HELP** fix it.

You stand up
for what is RIGHT.

You teach that **everyone MATTERS.**

You **PROTECT**
those who need it,
no matter how small.

Even when
things look
impossible . . .

and your goal seems
far away . . .

because you **CARE**!

And the rewards
can be
unexpected . . .
and priceless.

It's who you are
and what you do.
You are KIND!